In the Pink Arms of
the City

Also by Toni Thomas:

Chosen
    Brick Road Poetry Press

Fast as Lightening
    Gribble Press

Walking on Water
    Finishing Line Press

Blue Halo
    Annalese Press

Ace Raider of the Unfathomable Universe
    Annalese Press

You'll be Fast as Lightning Coveting my Painted Tail
    Annalese Press

Hotsy Totsy Ballroom
    Annalese Press

Love Adrift in the City of Stars
    Annalese Press

In the Pink Arms of the City

Poems

First published in 2019 by Annalese Press
134 Towngate
Netherthong
Holmfirth
West Yorkshire HD9 3XZ
England

Copyright © 2019 Toni Thomas

All rights reserved. No part of this publication may be reproduced, stored, or transmitted in any form, or by any means electronic, mechanical or photocopying, recording or otherwise, without the express written permission of the publisher.

Photograph by Toni Thomas
Cover design, layout and sketches by
Peter Wadsworth

British Library Cataloguing-in-Publication Data
A catalogue record for this book is available on request from the British Library.

ISBN 978-0-9956652-8-6

Acknowledgements

So many gifted poets have leant their generosity to my development, and for this I remain forever grateful. Very special thanks go to Galway Kinnell, Ilya Kaminsky, Sharon Olds, Brigit Pegeen Kelly, and Lucille Clifton who have inspired and mentored me in invaluable ways. Thank you Nikky Finney for your encouragement and Li-Young Lee for your gentle words.

Contents

Part One: *Along the Trellises of the Dark*

I walk streets that boast	5
I passed by happiness today	6
It is fortuitous to arrive here	7
We are handholding	8
In the pink arms of the city	9
I am not calling up friends	10
Evening	11
Edinburgh	12
I once thought I could remain	13
In the winding stretch of road	15
In the bay by the Almond River	16
In Holyrood Park	18
In the frozen alley	19

Part Two: *A Surfeit of Longing*

It is my seventh week in this city	25
The man smoking his cigar	28
Oktoberfest, Edinburgh	29
Five miles from here	31
The man one floor up laughs	32
In the corner store	34
Mr. Ike's dog died yesterday	35
At the bar of the Brass Horse Tavern	36
Past St. Cuthbert's Church	38
In the Botanical Garden	39
In Oban you can buy	40
The rooms are crowded in curios	41
The roads here	43

PART THREE: *In the Heart's Suitcase*

The large man is being helped up the steps	49
The man with the peeled skin	51
The neighbour next door	52
On the Leith Walk bus	54
The boy in Dysart	55
On the bus it is easy	56
Off the Royal Mile	57
Our hostess slides down	58
Off Dalry Road	60

PART FOUR: *Secret Happiness*

The sky hangs low	67
In Oban the sky mimics	68
Even when the river ran clear	69
The sun flirts today	70
The young woman in Musselburgh	72
Beside the deep waters of Loch Ness	73
The streets of Leith	74
Across the darkness	76
In my dream	78
In Cramond the five girls	80
In the Chocolatier Shop and Café, Oban	82
It is raining	84
These two love each other	85
On the glass panels	86
Somewhere beyond the waters of Loch Lomond	88

For you
My lucky palomino in the field

O that someday, with the passing of this grim vision,
I might sing out jubilant praise to assenting angels;
that of all the clear-struck keys of my heart, none
should fail on doubtful, slack or irascible strings;
that my streaming face might make me more radiant,
with an inconspicuous weeping bloom there. How dear
will you be to me then, you nights of sorrowing.
Oh why did I not, disconsolate sisters, kneel
more to receive you, give myself more loosely
into your loosened hair. We, spendthrifts of sorrows.

Rainer Maria Rilke
Tenth Elegy

Part One

Along the Trellises of the Dark

I walk streets that boast

bright tabled cafes, lit houses
Persian rugs, grilled sea bass, Argentine reds.
Someone in a flat deals cards
brews tea, folds laundry
reaches for the story of three bears
a boy plays with his dog
glow lamps wax stable
there is laughter, plump eiderdowns
easy sleep when night falls.

Not everyone lives like this
on more than empty
some of us carry the jars of the dead
are spring flowers without a home.

Is it true that what gets left behind
sometimes saves
that in the heart's lonely suitcase
silence can offer up
a breath more sonorous
spacious
than bread?

I passed by happiness today

gave it a wave.
Crumbs fell from a supplicate table.
The sun stood vacant.

Someone poured milk
flirted with bunt cake.
A billboard advertised love
as a pole dance.

Keep me safe I said
unsure if anybody listens.

Is it possible to banish people
by omission
as if no one is homeless
sleeps in a bedroll
needs us?

It is fortuitous to arrive here

where the afternoon light off the castle saves
and damp buns and cake
and posters for the Billy Elliot revival at the Strand
and old men pushing draughts at a pocket table
and the accordion lady with her mohawk and singsong
and the children whose cheeks resemble pudding
with smears of rose petal
where no one needs to offer a false note.

Up the street a kettle whistles
an old man sweeps his steps
the couple in the fifth floor walkup
pause in the middle of their lovemaking
up the street the kebab vendor slices lamb
a tram bell rings
schoolboys tuck into greasy chips, pizza

the world feels plausible
not threatened by climate change, loss
a tent city
bankrupt boat
cancer.

We are handholding

not young, not old
the sun threatens to shine
the art gallery offers up a corniced room
budget priced prints
ceramic cats, a small tray of biscuits.
Faces shine out bigger than money.

Even the soot on the street seems scrupulous
won't disturb the passersby
the people in the laundromat folding sheets
couple with the cappuccino, lemon cake
the man in his odd bowler hat
won't disturb the woman in yellow curls
leashed pug, the side stepped
center staged.

It is mid-September
this afternoon someone will climb Arthur's Seat
walk the Royal Mile
purchase a meat pie
buy milk, corn flakes
listen to fiddle music
walk unsteady with a cane.

We are handholding
the streets of Leith
as if we have a home, a room, hotplate
as if the sky stays loyal
our hearts won't drizzle

and we want to believe
just off Easter Road
the Polish couple in Lochend Park
are still dancing.

In the pink arms of the city

everything looks perky
the man eats his ham sandwich as he walks
a child recites *fair thee well my green field*
football bets are lost and won
beer mugs chime
in the midst of this mid-September morning
the memory of last night's fiddle music plays on.

In the pink arms of the city
I wear two sweaters to stay warm
watch the girly girl with pompoms
twirl in front of the shop window
as if she can smash the eye of the rain
always glitter.

I ride a double decker bus
across South Bridge, Royal Mile
watch tourists sample whiskey
disappear down Princes Street
become abbreviation
pint size dots
half spent, homecoming.

In the pink arms of the city
I become the girl who hides in cafes
wordless
lives on cereal and bread
doesn't want to mercantile her life
with a lock and key
razor image for money.

I am not calling up friends

to tell them the news
being homeless does something
pares things down
next meal, warm bed, stay dry
find a locker, job, cheap phone
address.

In the normal course of our days
do we take things for granted -
Sunday roast, craft beer
live music, talk of Prague, Brittany
the economy, investment portfolio
how to posture ourselves pretty?

It is easy to imagine other people's lives
the happiness they grow
pass by windows, look inside
framed art, velvet armchairs
plates of cheese, watercress, new potato

easy to remember the glow of
gas lamps on Marchmont
the fruit vendor, patisserie
displays of raspberry tart, gateau
mannequins wrapped in cashmere
the fish monger
slabs of red meat in the butcher's window

the way the world shines jeweled
no pock marks
prison suicide, blighted crop
as if we are perpetually prized
at home
acceptable.

Evening

Some rooms are rooms
faraway
we go to them
with our eyes dim.
To eat at their table
is an act of parsimony.

I have known rooms like this
where sacrifice limps
love is a tape measure.

Speak to me then as if you
really mean it
as if light never fails
the woman down the road
dying for lack of bread
means something to you.

Edinburgh

It is autumn
the city stares back
satisfied
people buy tartan plaid, cashmere
malt whisky
restaurants are full
plates of oyster
steak, lamb, haggis
fancy desert cake
Bavarian chocolate.

But sometimes the wind grows thrifty
the season of gift giving escapes
there are vacant rooms
broken bells
sunlight clipped by a cold stranger

we travel a bare ocean
the view is thin
I carry my house on my back
work to stretch hope
into a river.

I once thought I could remain

clueless
never need to hold
a bird by the throat
make it sing
that the night wears
flaming pajamas
a nest egg

thought I could duck in and out
walk a thin line through border country
that my children's hands cup blue bells
a bright ring

thought the punctuation of rain
was mere preamble
everyone is granted a roof
predilection, meal plan
some manner of nosegays

that our folk songs -
 for fair green meadows we sing
 for Abigails and jonquil
 and the laurels of Spring
are a shared birthright.

I once thought nobody goes without
a country, a home
our hands hold Paris and palm trees
unsubscribed sand
swim in an opal ocean

the orphaned boy gets adopted
rides the surf in a float tube.

I once thought that along the trellises of the dark
walk deathless roses
a surfeit of singing.

In the winding stretch of road

up from Carlyle toward Edinburgh
cows meander across
the wide sweep of fields
as if they are careless
intent to chew grass, watch the sky
let the rope of their tails swing
even as pendulums.

I am glad to see the cows grazing on
the loose bowl of hills beyond Biggen
beyond its market square and puppet theatre
as if their lives are an open river
scenery of bright foliage
as if these Cumbrian farmers
are in love with the earth's creatures
knows how to caretake

as if agribusiness is only a fiction
some futuristic pot boiler
thousands of miles away.

In the bay by the Almond River

sailboats slump
festooned with mud
now that the sea has rescinded
left them in a bondage of seaweed
border country.

I have been marooned like this
when time rushes
and the life I once knew is elsewhere.

In the bay where the Firth meets
the Almond River
the tide is low
as if even river water gives up
we are a punctuation of tides
variance.

Once while my brother and I watched
from shore
my mother swam so far out to sea
we thought she would disappear
become the speck of magenta
dotting a dark ocean.

I wanted to believe nothing perishes
not boats, a mother, house, family
that we are dancing otters
in a benevolent sea
God saves
no one is permanently beached
discarded as useless.

That day my mother turned shoreward
came back
then in another season

abruptly went away
as if her heart could no longer live here
as if no measure of love or money
can anchor a broken emissary.

In Holyrood Park

the world looks sane
no one is deterred
forced to dance a jig
join a ceilidh

propositions fit
the woman who begs on
Princes Street is far away.

In Hollyrood Park
to speak the truth
won't maim
be viewed as betrayal
the inflammatory pen rising

even the banned weed
gypsum
fern and fuchsia
have their unruly truths to tell
won't buckle their lips shut
when we pass.

In the frozen alley

the people with no houses
give their lives up to newspaper
kindling, matchsticks
flasks of black tea.

This city has no place for them
is gutted with high rent
house sales turned into a bid war.

I have seen tired faces huddle
by an open flame, feel lost
children nurse bread
dogs grow empty.

In the frozen alley
of the grand city
where Arthur's Seat lives
in the shadow of an ancient castle
in the antique air

the roomless people wait
huddle around their card game
knapsack, bedroll

the poet perishes
the best of us is given away.

Part Two

A Surfeit of Longing

It is my seventh week in this city

living provisional
my suitcase lodged in budget rooms with
other people's shaving cream
penthouse pinups, shampoo.
And I think of those folks who navigate homeless
vie with strangers for an affordable flat
must show off gleaming credentials, a blonde wig.
But this is not me
I am not doing well
have sores in my mouth
live on scribble pads, bread, instant soup.

And I remember the divorce six years ago
his strategic smooth talk with attorneys
the claim I made less money so I should be
the one exiting the family home
my stuff thrown into a storage locker
the way he stood over me impudent as a hawk
to be sure I took only the poetry, fiction
that was mine not his from the book shelves
and I remember the feeling of family home
to homeless
my two children still back there safe
hiding in their rooms to stay out of the crossfire
trying to find a rental place with enough room
for two kids, two dogs
one that had central heat, a yard space
not an open sore they would hate compared to
the combed neighborhood.

And I remember that summer
finally finding a landlord
who would work with me, my marginal salary
as an adjunct college teacher
the rundown pintsize house in Oregon City

how my teenage daughter and I moved in
painted every dark sickly toned room
bright light colors
only to find out later, come mid-September
when she said *I am cold*
that there was no central heat
the walls thin and unlined as cardboard.

And I remember weekends crying alone
in the frigid house
wrapped up in blankets on the old futon
crying and crying about the state of our lives
so much loss
what it feels like to be near homeless
sell everything of value
including my mother's antique wedding ring
in order to pay utility bills, high school fees
buy groceries, gas
buy my daughter a used bed, dresser, wardrobe

and I remember my father
when I asked him for help saying –
somebody needs to break you of your dependency
as if the recession, high rent
my husband's betrayals
the choice to marry him
this predicament I was living in
was my own fault and like America
I was being told to buck up
find a way back onto some dubious success ladder
by the state of my own volition
survive

and how some of us, like my father
can take a life made out of nothing
and a childhood orphanage
manage to rise up into the army
then government work
save, be a student, marry a woman who dies
then another
have a life, house, trips to Europe
in the public eye not seem to leak
the blue-eyed boy wounds of his heart
how my mother's heart in his shadow will fail
and she will die young

how not all of us have the same stamina
to survive the cards that are dealt to us –
call us tenuous, fragile, call us dreamers
call us doers of good work, poets of the heart
a delicate wind attempting to navigate
a razored landscape
call us America's failures, America's forgotten

and for forty nine days
I have been here in Edinburgh
magnificent city that it is
thinking about homelessness
feeling so very provisional
wanting to believe it is not all about commerce
that only the most aggressive survive.

The man smoking his cigar

at the café table
along the Stromania
does not bother anyone

but still the trail of smoke insists
billows under the blue awning
travels to your table, mine
sets up camp
a hazy landscape
reminds me of board rooms
poker playing in Reno
train cars, men's clubs
the inscrutable.

The man in pressed slacks
has a mastery over his face
his companion wears silk stockings
alligator heels
appears pert, preserved
as if nothing very bad
ever happens in their world.

When did I grow weary of prerogative
the blasé words and the ballsy?

Oktoberfest, Edinburgh

Double size steins laden with foam
are being passed around
as lederhosen clad, middle aged band musicians
sing *Going to stay at the YMCA*
and *Saturday night fever*
to the shrieks of the twenty year olds
packed tight inside the canvas tent
along dozens of plank tables set in orderly rows.

The college crowd plays at Bavarian
they stand up on tabletops, wooden benches
swing their steins, costumed bodies
gyrate and sing.
It is still early.
The wait staff are young, pert and cater.

The pretty girl next to me is dressed in
an old fashioned gingham dress, cotton apron
finishes the look with a classic wool sweater
expensive pumps, plaited hair
has two companions in white poufy shirts
suspenders, shorts, feathered alpine caps
and I marvel at the sheer variety
from lacy low cut bosomy blouses to fishnet
wool vests, go-go boots, knee highs.

The massive canvas tent rolls.
All the American tunes are being played.
There are plates of chips, sausage, kraut
giant pretzels tossed in rock salt.

And I think back to last weekend
the area up in Perthshire we drove through
where a chunk of the population are out of work

where the newspaper talks about local hospitals
on the verge of closing
and I think of my father 3,000 miles away
telling me on the phone how he is determined
to make it to the Oktoberfest at Mt. Angel

take in the accordion music, yodeling, folk dances
even if it means three buses, two hours each way
after all, he was stationed in Germany during the war
and at 88-years-old, even if nobody is saying
there's always the risk this might be the last.

Here in the tent back in Edinburgh
the band musicians are singing
Welcome to the Hotel California
and the crowd goes crazy
hoists themselves back up on the tables
everyone stomps, sways
chugs down more beer.

Five miles from here

a man escaped his life yesterday
on a train track.
Some things are too gruesome
all I know is that it was rush hour
the track barrier arms were down
the red light flashing.

He had a wife, two kids
job, flat, reasons to be here.

Is there a limit to our obduracy
the daily scramble, buses
ticket taking, shop carts
boxed sandwiches
easy rhetoric, repetitive

did the man wake up one day
to a different voice
memorize trees
the sky's hymnal
night dreams

did he and his wife kiss
were the bills a burden
did his boss know him as
more than replaceable
a bright gem in a sea of plastic?

What will the school say
when the man never arrives back
to pick up his kids
how will the wife sleep now that a
blank space invades her bed
what will the dark say about blindness
the heart's broken fuselage?

The man one floor up laughs

as if the roof will rise
talks brilliant politics
cups his four-year-old son's yellow curls
wants to save the world
as one glass of red wine after the next
is passed around
till he is the only one refilling his glass.

He is from Ireland, tells me his father
was once an architect
died young so his mother raised them.

The man has lived a life of curiosity
thinks out of the box, tells grand stories
is in his late 50's, has a part-time job
get-away two room house in Greece
likes family sun holidays –
Sicily, the Canary Islands, Morocco.

When you leave him there is a warm glow
his young son says -
my father wakes up singing old hits.
He is loved by his children, wife
doesn't go to the local pub anymore
drink with his mates, says –
we are busy raising kids, being a family
but I wonder deep down what his children
are learning about wine's sweet patronage
its ruby color, the way it turns river
incites bright stories
dazzles the dark
can make for a sharp jab
center stage, flushed face

wonder whether when the door shuts
when his lovely wife wipes off her mascara
slides into a nightgown
attempts to soothe
she tastes a perilous and
secret kind of weeping.

In the corner store

they don't trust our fingers
as if we pinch things
the wrapped candies in the bins -
carmel crèmes, dainty suzies, macaroons
vanilla bean beasties, chocolate palavers.
My mum says the owner is on to us
that if we don't behave we'll never succeed
warns that my appetite is mule size
taints virtue
nobody wants a boy who takes.

To this end I play good boy
turn the other cheek
shovel the chicken shit in our yard
burn trash, sweep porch
lecture myself blue
when we enter the corner store
keep my hands anchored.

See how I store up good grades
till I am the crowd pleaser
velvet my words, table talk
hold my pinky around the spoon
become more than juvenile
a boatload of knowledge
arbiter of shame.

Mr. Ike's dog died yesterday

of heart failure
had an oatmeal coat
half terrier, pixie.
I never saw the dog run for a ball
roll on her back.

The old man is 86
walks with a catheter
blasts the TV cause his hearing is shot
forgets his oven till the meat smokes

plays bridge with a handful of seniors
hauls food from the Star Market
hobbles with his walker, plastic bags
while the light turns
the cars wait.

Mr. Ike's dog died yesterday
more sudden than low income rooms go missing
lovers get lost or found.
Her name was Lacey.
They'd been together a lot of years.
In winter he'd wrap an old red sweater
around her midsection.

But death happens every day here
things come and go
you get used to it.

At the bar of the Brass Horse Tavern

you can order up amber ale
the blue plate special, haggis
pasties and pints.
The woman down the end hums
Crossing the Minch, sips red wine
an old man stares out the window
flame crackles under the weight of the logs.

The man in the peaked cap
nurses his pint
hasn't treated his wife badly
murdered his sister
swindled children
but still the luck of St. Cuthbert
refuses to come home.

He is waiting for someone
doesn't know he is waiting
why sometimes his heart folds over
threatens to empty.

It's Thursday.
At 9pm the musician arrives
sets up his fiddle, bar stool
starts to sing about the old country
Loch Lomond, shipwrecks
the Maid of Islay
about broken love
sheepherders, a blue brothel.

The man in the tweed cap shouts for the one
about the mountains of home
knows the words
raises his craggy voice into chorus -

there shall I visit the place of my birth
they'll give me a welcome the warmest on earth
so loving and kind, full of music and mirth,
the sweet sounding language of home

hail to the mountains with summits of blue
to the glens with their meadows of sunshine and dew
to the women and the men ever constant and true
ever ready to welcome me home

sings it as if he is waiting on something
as if the world holds no plastic
gets up, goes over to the bar
orders himself another drink.

Past St. Cuthbert's Church

the graveyard
shadowed tombstones, damp air
a man waits for the bus
beneath a glass shelter
has a port wine birthmark
that moves paisley across his face.

And I am reminded of Janie
from so many years ago
whose family I saw at the children's center.
Janie of the single parent household with three kids
whose mom worked swing shift at a nursing home
was always trying to find decent childcare.
Janie with the thick black hair, chestnut eyes
big toothed smile who was pressed too
by a birthmark that fingered halfway across her face
had set up a dance there.

She was eleven years old.
Kids can say cruel things
about what they don't understand.
She knew name calling
a mother unschooled in talking to employers
healthcare providers
driving a car
pro bono surgeries, laser treatment.

Ahead of Janie was the peer pressure of high school
the way looking different feels
in a spotless world.

In the Botanical Garden

my daughter fingers the blue gentian
her brother runs ahead through the stand of sitka
that speak of firm roots, crowns that will outlive us.
I drink coffee, search for a restroom.
Inside the garden café families sit, talk
eat roast beef, mashed potato, pudding
the menu is not cheap but tempts.
We settle for two brioche.
A couple on the bridge want me to take their picture.
They are young, in love with themselves, each other
and I remember back to my own days of torrid lovemaking
when tepid was never enough
before the children
before my husband found other women
late night emails
before my days of single parenthood.
My son points to a vendor with paper birds
they flap their wings on a string as if nothing abandons us.
My daughter moans *I am tired of walking.*

It is Sunday.
The Botanical Garden teams with visitors.
My coffee is still in my hand, half drunk, cold.
There is a moratorium on pain.
September and fine weather can do this.
The test gardens lined with red cabbage
salad greens, chard, leeks, onion
remind me of our beds, row after row
behind the farmhouse in the Coast Range
when nothing seemed spoilable
and America swung on its golden dream
before things turned a different color
before my children and I were homeless
and everything began to run ragged in the wind.

In Oban you can buy

saltwater taffy, local chocolate
dine on sea scallops from Mull
big as your palm
buy a wood plaque that reads
the sea gives, the sea takes away.

Workers with lined faces
make feed for farmed salmon, trout.
The fish live in pens
are bred to grow quick
sickless
be iced, shipped off
later breaded, batter fried
grilled for our tables.

And I wonder about their lives
a fish's natural rhythm
the thousands of miles back to a birthplace
the deposit of eggs
instinct
how a natural cycle gets interrupted
what it means

and yesterday I read in the newspaper
about tons of farmed trout
escaped off a Norwegian ship
rammed by a tanker
the way they spilled into the lap
of a dark ocean
swam away swiftly
how other boats were radio alerted
to act quick
retrieve what was salvageable.

The rooms are crowded in curios

she wants a blank space on the third shelf
place for a Hummel
boy with a peaked cap, blue shirt
who wanders the Bavarian hills
is a younger version of my father
but with peach toned skin
parents who love.

Some rooms keep their past shrouded
are trophied mantles, powder puffs
a bronze version of first booties.

Some lives were never made to order
must run on their own volition
keep the wind from pilfer
find their own way to buy eyeglasses
a steady meal, schoolbooks.

Maybe like the old woman next door
I have spent my life rearranging rooms
managing their pitfalls
blue inertia
their pauper shoes, scream fits
the way they attempt to codify Christmas
after the mother drops dead.

The woman in the flat next door
will never know my father
cross paths with him
his spent dreams, hard life
never know how some boys turn

blue as an orphanage
no longer believe the sky reigns down
bright ponies
reliable lovers
a durable kiss.

The roads here

hold pert houses
white stucco
or weathered stone.
The Chinese restaurant
serves Szechuan chicken, teardrop soup
rice noodles, reopens at five.
In the café an older couple
sits before plates of black pudding, tatties
eggs, bacon, their coffee comes with a side mint
is strong and black, just as they ask.

Some people stroll, some rush.
There is no rain.
It is a Saturday in October
the economy is stable
advertised flats go quick
the red Lothian buses move timely
the two girls seated in front are from Naples
people speak in Polish, French
Czech, English, Farsi.
The stops are even and the bus driver will sell
you a ticket on board for the right coin.

It's easy to be subdued by this
the coach seats to Glasgow
their trim grey cloth, polished windows
believe the world never rusts, deserts us
the sun grinds in place
the field confers unsprayed courgettes, lettuce
the food is good
museums boast European art
the history of tenements
scrap metal sells for a pound at the Barra Market
easy to believe the foliage of autumn stays glued

no one has a black and blue face
scares us.

It's easy to board this bus
admit no warfare, no shrapnel.
No one dies in a refugee camp
crosses a perilous ocean.

Our houses are tidy, our pastimes endless.
Today Indian summer smothers with a warm coat
like yesterday and the day before
passersby will be curious about my black and blue face
discreet when our eyes meet, turn politely away.

I will half want to explain about the broken nose
the way you shame things
how my heart is a small exhibit
in a wax museum
turned invalid
ancient
to survive.

Part Three

In the Heart's Suitcase

The large man is being helped up the steps

into the Black Friar Pub
by what are probably his wife and brother.
They are patient, solicitous
joke about the football match
lamb shank on the menu, the number of steps
lack of rain.
The man is very slow
will be happy to arrive indoors
be arranged at one of the tables.

I am reminded of my cousin, Emma
the dimpled princess age five
who will lose her father that year to a heart attack -
no life insurance, four children and a tired mom.
Emma who wants to be an elementary school teacher
learns to play the trumpet in school band
earns a degree in early ed at the state university
comes back home to stay afterwards
because the teaching jobs are out of state
and her mother will be left alone if she takes one.

Emma who will end up paper pushing insurance claims
later factory office work, never marry, have kids
never leave the worn down pintsize ranch house
never once complain, show regret
because love is thick
and she loves her mother.
Emma who will nurse my aunt nights after work
till the day she goes into her final stay in the hospital.

Perhaps this is the knot that binds
drives deep into the family that loves
this lastness
that holds the glue
cements

rounds the hard edges
insures the man with the walker
who travels inch by inch
very unsteady
will know a night out
sit across from the spitting fire
sip his dram of whiskey
tuck into the menu's decent roast
know company, laughter
companionship that saves.

The man with the peeled skin

isn't looking at anyone
his face stares out the bus window
or straight ahead.
And I think of the world I am living in –
our differences, our sames
what it must mean to hold
a rare and strange bird in your palm
not flinch, run away.

The man with the peeled skin on his face
has probably known school jokes
hospital surgeries
hard pain
may have a lover, family
decent job, warm flat

or else be secretly looking for these
as if it is our shared wishes that bind us
our hopes, sorrow
that have nothing to do with a smooth face
the nature of skin.

To bridge this distance seems to me
to know god in street clothes
riding an everyday bus.

The neighbour next door

feeds her husband his afternoon toast.
He is in his blue cotton pajamas
has a bib tied round his neck
as if sometimes things slip away.
Their place is compact, homey, well combed.
They sleep in the same room, in separate
mirror image beds with identical throws.

I am early, here to look at a flat
she heard me fumbling, invites me in
shows me their cutaway kitchen wall
that gives the illusion of more space
talks about the tide
view out their pocket window
the cheese shop in Portobello
afternoon tribe of sailboats tacking.

They look like they have been together
a long time
as if love binds
loyalty has no death wish
won't stone down the door
insist a timetable.

She offers me tea then goes back
to feeding her husband his toast
from a makeshift tray table.
The man mentions the weather
mumbles that the apartment needs paint
maybe next spring.
It is not easy to understand him.
She tells me that downstairs
on the lawn there's a drying line
yard shed we get to share

and I am reminded of longevity
the way her patient hands speak
do not rush out the door
as if something vague but tangible
a dance hall, romp in the grass
stroll down the beach
are missing.

On the Leith Walk bus

tiredness wears loose trousers
uncombed hair
a bagged bread roll
backpacks and plastic
black tea, potato.

I sit cocooned as the
stops come and go
remember a date night
my child's first birthday
the Black Cuillin on Skye
finger foods for the deceased

remember that evening in Dunkeld
when the musician stopped playing his fiddle
long enough to walk
the blind woman home.

The boy in Dysart

ties a nylon line around his ankle
so he can feel the tug
fishes for mackerel, dogfish
whatever will bite
says he uses a shiny spinner
it always works

tells me he and his friend
once caught eight mackerel in two hours
that dog fish have the yank of a truck
shellfish bring in the quid.

The harbor is quiet
good weather, early October
a handful of strollers
the remains of a Cistercian monastery.
On the beach two toddlers dig sand
a dog runs for a stick.

The boy tells me he once caught
a rare butterfly, let it go
that lobsters fetch ten quid apiece
but he has no boat, bait traps.

With the nylon line tied to the boy's leg
I chide him about the strength of a dogfish
whether it will carry him off fast as a jet boat
but he giggles in a bluster of confidence -
could never happen
I feel every nibble on the line
am ready for anything!

On the bus it is easy

to rehearse life
not grow ruthless
sit and read
check out the car strewn scenery
imagine the person next to you
is a newfound friend, lover
marry the before and afters.

On the bus it is possible to
be handed the perfect cozy flat
right man, marriage.
Children adore you.
The weather holds out.
The evening ahead is good –
curried cauliflower and rice.

Every glance between strangers
feels like a love note.

Off the Royal Mile

it is easy to forget about money
the way it struts in a rain storm
offers up champagne and oysters.

This is the city that breathes
ancient stone, a king's seat
brooding castle
will invite you to fiddle music
haggis, drams of whiskey.

But if longing were a shy bird
what would it say to us
about bounty, the burning bush
a king's ransom
about the hands of crofters
scarcity of bread
how the homeless mother fields a coin
with her tipped hat, bedroll.

Whoever carried the cross
up Calvary are they already here
lost in the back streets beyond Leith
Gorgie, the Dalry?

Our hostess slides down

plates of breakfast
black pudding, eggs, sausage, bacon
hash browns, a full tray of toast
stalls happiness at our door.
Her children need her.
Two girls thirteen and seventeen that have
been through their share
the father drinking himself to death
the hard time in Glasgow
the new man who refurbishes motorcycles
stuffs a slew of them in the barn as trophy.

The breakfast is good
the old farmhouse renovated
fancy rooms for tourists on the second floor.
She tells me how she was raised inside a bakery
her parents owned it for 25 years on the Isle of Mull
but after the death of her mother
her father's two heart attacks
he's moved over here, takes her daughter to school
has a studio flat up by the infirmary.

And her father pokes his head into the breakfast room
with its new butcher-block tables, vase of silk roses
a ruddy looking man, white haired, jovial
tells us about his life as a baker
the good spring wheat they shipped from Canada
how it held the right amount of gluten
made the bread elastic
not like *that insipid winter wheat variety*
and how one of the local lads came to apply for a job
had been manning machines on a factory floor
and the workers there went on strike when the boss

threatened to cut their break time
since it was the only thing they ever looked forward to
that and lunch

and he explained to the lad about the bakery job
how working the flour, kneading the loaves
taking from the earth to the grain mill
to the flour boards and bake oven
folks coming in day after day
and then coming back for more
is different from machinery
does something to a person
satisfies the soul
told the lad he'd know more reward in the bakery
than just a break time

and now he lives near Inverness
tells us there's still such a thing as good work
that he misses Mull, the bakery
wishes us fair travel

and afterwards my breakfast holds even greater light
as I pause over the fields of spring wheat
see the baker's hands kneading the dough
spread his daughter's bright orange marmalade
across the toast.

Off Dalry Road

the neighborhood cafe
holds parked metal walkers, canes
out of work people snugged behind newspapers
a child with yellow ringlets, stringy terrier
the woman who drinks coffee
tends her feeble daughter strapped in a wheelchair.
The girl looks about twelve, never speaks
 has creamy skin others might envy.

Someone is having vegetable soup in a white bowl
dunks in the bread
there are racks of handmade Christmas cards
with white doves, Mary, a river
Fair Trade felted purses, thick scones
jam that boasts of summer strawberries, a pear tree.

In the neighborhood café
a big man sits at the table across from me.
He has come in to join his friend
has arms laced with tattoos, skin piercings
clothes that remind me life is not easy.
Mothers wheel in babies, push strollers with
stuffed sheep, wrapped sausage
carrot, milk cartons, potato
search for a naptime, tea break, chat.

Thanks to the big windows, a sheet of skylight
nothing feels closed in
reduced to a cramped life
bare bones hotel room.
The folks that work here are older
men and women who keep the faith
take orders, money
make the sandwiches, do dishes, serve.
Prices are more than reasonable.

Along the street sit repair shops
the closed metal door of the Tandoori
St. Matthews Church
a beauty salon that also does nails
batter fried chicken, takeout pizza
the children's nursery dotted with bamboo screens
a tiny clubhouse, grow garden, bake kitchen.
A boy rides his blue scooter while his mother walks
couples wander, the man with the leather jacket
moves unsteady
stops to gaze in the pawn shop window
then winds his way back toward a pub.

In the back of the café two men
grill cheese sandwiches, hose down plates.
They have soft lined faces, busy hands
will bus your table, wipe with a cloth.
The grey haired women at the front
take coffee orders, speak in bird language
serve up the cake, soup, tea, cookies.
Customers look comfortable, familiar around them.

Tell me, is there a certain decency better than wealth?

PART FOUR

Secret Happiness

Part Two

The sky hangs low

not like the heavy twin blood clots that
have infested my father's leg
but still damning
still testament that even the sun on a mission
will have a hard time breaking through today.

Are some lives hastened
by this kind of grey
reduced to canes and corner shops
to pork pie, a one room flat

or still in their faithful
do they have covenants to keep
mount buses, walk toddlers
stew potato
empty dumpsters
collect trash
keep their timecards faithful
keep a pint sized version of the sun
stashed in their pocket?

Today on a bus into Southbridge
the baby in the stroller sits drowned
in the love of her Polish grandmother.
Blankets are arranged, rearranged
giggles exchanged, fingers twined
ringlets fussed with
a garland of pink satin buds
fastened around her head
as if already she needs to prove nothing
like you and me
is priceless.

In Oban the sky mimics

the slur of the field
inimitable grey is more than
the eye of the beholder.

She is cooking us breakfast
in her B&B kitchen
with the bright red enamel.
It is showcase perfect, boasts
a giant American style frig/freezer.

Her black pudding comes from the Shetlands
there is beef cake, pork sausage, eggs
a rack of toast, marmalade.
Nobody goes hungry.

Her husband drives truck
rolls in on Fridays
comes home to a pert blonde
good stories, ceramic cats
band practice
date nights

to a woman who knows how to fix things
make a man anxious to hurry back
raises a daughter to adulthood so loyal
she moves only three houses away.

Even when the river ran clear

there was still a mill
skeins of yarn, weavers' cottages
women whose eyes strained
whose hands knew taut thread
a third floor stretch of window
distances.

They worked long hours in poor light
wove our socks, sweaters, gloves
kept the looms clicking.
To be a weaver's daughter was
to be apprenticed to factories
spring wool, spinning, carding
the stain of dyes
eye strain, blue spectacles.

They say over the course of years
Helen R. wove a record 1,365 sweaters
for a mill up by Slaithwaite
before the arthritis claimed her.

The sun flirts today

may or may not land on our shoulders
serenade the grass, make the cat dozy.
Last night's beach fire turned to
charred board, ember
the Portobello shore sprinkled in ash pits
a promenade thick with
Sunday passersby, coffee.

I don't always know my way around
how to find a handhold, a place
carry my words in a cradle.

The sun flirts today
might become a willing mother
importune man gone off in a caravan
blue swale.

By noon people peel off jackets
remember where they have been
where they are heading.
I run my hand along the fine bones
of your face, know their decency.
The sun dozes then flirts, reminds me
this is no season for regret
charred wood, a shrew heart.

I want to be here
sometimes don't know how
want a room, a job, life
not to go missing
be invisible.
Remember I am homeless
but my heart is not.
The gulls of the dark seep
God hangs on a thin thread.

Along the narrow band of beach
children play ball, run
gather sand in their shoes.

I am not alone.

The young woman in Musselburgh

eats fish out of newspaper.
The day is a wash of loose vowels
puppies play in the waves, magpies pilfer
the sun scribbles
and in the Firth of Forth
half a dozen sailboats are leaning.

Is it easy to love the world
your life, your body
on a day in October like this one
to wage no war
exact no end games

when nothing seems gutted
the sky rests in a blue plantation
mirrors the sea
children tag behind grownups
suck ice cream
shopkeepers offer up blue cheese, bread loaf
glasses of burgundy, tartan plaids
whiskey.

Beside the deep waters of Loch Ness

low lying mist
burdens the afternoon hillside.
Someone hammers metal
fishes for pike
holds a grandchild
stirs porridge
opens the eyelet hooks of a dress.

Some of us hold our secrets
like a winter bride
it will not be easy to tame us.

Scratch two sticks
flame the birch kindle
open a drawer
the blue commode
that holds secret happiness
no public applause
is palpable as a delicate bird
shyly dim as your nightshade.

The streets of Leith

speak of folks in hoodies
couples, families
mothers and strollers
fish vendors, kebab
a slim pantry of potato.

We are handholding
not young, not old
attempt to forgive each other's trespasses
the sun threatens to shine
the art gallery offers up a corniced room
budget priced prints
ceramic cats, a small tray of biscuits.
Faces shine out bigger than money.

Even the soot on the street seems scrupulous
won't disturb the passersby
the people in the laundromat folding sheets
couple with the cappuccino, lemon cake
the man in his odd bowler hat
won't disturb the woman in yellow curls
leashed pug, the side stepped
center staged.

It is late October
this afternoon folks will climb Arthur's Seat
walk the Royal Mile
purchase a meat pie
buy milk, frosted flakes
listen to fiddle music
walk unsteady with a cane.

We are handholding
the streets of Leith

as if we have a home, a room, hotplate
as if the sky stays loyal
our hearts won't drizzle

want to believe
that just off Easter Road
the Polish couple in Lochend Park
are still dancing.

Across the darkness

across the cobbles
carriages roll
hold perforated windows
a view of the field
hold people with canes
bleary eyed toddlers
a leashed dog
short man who sells newspapers.

The woman with the swan's neck
leans on her husband
a boy dozes
old folks clutch groceries
the teenager in pin curls fingers
her patent leather purse
unnamed suitcase.

They are tired
grateful for the ride
anxious to find stilts
a sturdy handrail, hot toddy
steady room with a hot plate.

Do some of us need a hand
a vessel
to not perish
realize our greatness?

Across the darkness
carriages carry people
heedless
along the pebbled road.
I do not know where they are heading

who will step off, get on
if the weather will be noble, the food decent
cost of concessions bearable.

Some futures are unknowable
like wheeled carriages they travel
beyond our conceit, second guesses
beyond the past and cheap rhetoric
dream a sky cradle, new home
host family
workshop of birds.

In my dream

you wear autumn
hold the persistence of a sea merchant
search continents
blue amphibian, booty.
If we crossed paths, were strangers
I know I'd be taken by you
convinced that you never scare dogs
tame wallpaper into ruin.

We are on a bus to Glasgow
your voice is soft
you point out Arthur's Seat
intricate light and shadow across a concrete garage
St. Matthew's Gothic steeple
the Scottie pup
fused glass gallery
factory kitchen busy with bread baking
the boy in the yellow mac
old couple handholding
and I am taken by your recital of small details
ones that are human, fallible
don't always last.

In Glasgow we visit the Barras market, museums.
You gobble a meat pasty
buy old photographs, postcards
an antique pocket knife that holds tweezers
tell me about your new sketches.

I am a good listener
rub your neck in the cafe
watch your eyes travel the dessert tray

cornice work, stained glass door
couples and families eating

wonder whether you have always
summoned the invisible
managed to get porpoise to fly
fit the unruly world
into your finely etched glass
beyond weeping?

In Cramond the five girls

wear identical grey blazers
crowd into a booth
order pizza, chips
don't yet know luckless days
the world without home or money.

And I remember back then
wearing a uniform
the shapeless maroon plaid
penny loafers
so no one appeared different
and God would always recognize us.

In Cramond the sun is a sickle
cuts the sea
makes the gulls squint
the picnic tables gather light and potato chips.
It is low tide, the sailboats slumped
as if the waters of the Firth
have abandoned them.

The girls in the booth giggle
talk Saturday's soccer game
the movie picture at the Odeon
facebook, twitter
chat about Mary T.
her mouth full of braces
the way she kisses up to the Latin tutor.
Back then I barely spoke.
The Catholic uniforms made our legs stumpy.
I was fifteen, wanted shape
wanted boys looking through the microscope
with me in biology class
not just a glimpse of them once a week
across the pews of a chapel.

The girls in my study hall liked gossip
could be mean, backbite
I grew quiet around them.

When we moved to New Hampshire
the end of my freshman year
and I was asked where I wanted to go
I condemned the school uniform class
the god worship in a glass jar
begged for pedestrian
said – *put me among the rabble*
as if ordinary rooms, mixed gender
holey jeans, ruffled sweaters, suede boots
had their infinite stories to tell

wanted to learn about backseat
movie dates at the drive-in
the Barbizon Beauty School
grinding our bodies at the school dance
wanted to learn how to peroxide my hair blonde
about bare midriffs and short shorts

about the way the world can seem dispossessed
ragged as a country field
where God rides reckless
where sin has no label
is not just cut glass
a blue sermon
won't fit in our identical lunchboxes

where night answers our bodies
with a kiss.

In the Chocolatier Shop and Café, Oban

Today a little whale slid into my coffee
hinged onto the back of my spoon
disappeared below the brown sea
began to melt
swale of dark chocolate, mocha ocean

and I worked to retrieve
worked to retrieve
being the working class girl that I am
afraid of windfalls, escape
remembered my foil covered chocolate coins
that disappeared years ago down
a Queens sewer grate

tried to retrieve my melting whale
till the side of my hand was coal stained
and the saucer became a graveyard
for beached whales
the chocolate a sludge heap
that no longer resembled anything.

This is how disappearance happens
café surprises turn into an aborted gift.

See how I eye you in the saucer
spend my apologies on your neglect
half want to spoon your lump of a body
back into the cup
dissolve you
till I am dark with cacao from Ecuador
ripe from the hands of the workers

the vats and hooks and crème and spin
am a dark, loquacious woman
who lures men into more than a coffee cup.

Like the whale you slide in then melt
till half remorse I scoop you out
rescue
lick you silly between the spoon
and my hot lips.

It is raining

does it always rain in the heart
before love saves

before the cat arrives
from her street walk
the child comes home to stay

before the ocean is more than
its tides
sardines
a checkbook.

It is raining.
I open my mouth
my coat
buttoned pantomimes

see how razored hope feels
uneven future
visited by rain.

These two love each other

walk down along the harbor of Oban
on a day ink blotted with clouds
no rain, no wind
no one in a hurry.

And the man will probably never be hurried.
It is not easy for him to walk but he is walking
moves up and down on uneven legs.
They are hand in hand, talk as they go.
She has hair the color of bleached wheat
a quilted jacket
his is brown, flecked with grey.

These two love each other.
It is no bother for her to walk slow for him.
If they never hike up a trail, straddle the river
she will not choose to resent.
In the morning he brings her tea, marmalade, biscuits.
They live in a bungalow, nurse secret trellises
no one else sees.

On the glass panels

of the bus shelter along Princes Street
rain is dancing
concentric circles, a steady pattern
like the paint dappled canvas
riffs from a punctuated piano

as if somewhere up above a sky god sings
the grey veil cracks
everything becomes phantasmagorical
the day with its bent umbrellas
wet shoes, red sided buses
is smashed with love
moist with kisses

and I who have never liked rain or grey
fled from it
sit here in the wide windowed café
astonished at my own blindness.

I tell you down below
the rain is making a ceremony
pats the streets clean
greens the trees
lands on rain macs, cotton jackets, hoodies
on bicyclists, wheelchairs
on men carrying briefcases, women with strollers
on the boy hauling a cardboard box
the school teen in blue blazer
dances a scherzo
on the glass panels of the bus stop

as old people wait, couples chatter
life carries on its ordinary Thursday.

Tell me, if we are composed mostly of water
are we destined to send out
our wet, slippery tears and kisses
make the leaves glisten, the plants perk up
moisten the dirt into pond swell and river
washcloth the day
become seminal with our own rainmaking?

Somewhere beyond the waters of Loch Lomond

the meandering road, stone fence
pork pies, tam o' shanters
beyond the kilts
fiddle fused shot glasses, amber ale
small impasses

beyond the cattle calls
damp carbon of what's been
what's about to happen

beyond the Blue Shepherd Pub
the man with the birth marked face

past all of this
in that silent space
I will meet you
where words fall loose
and a jig plays

where all of us are being called home
through the fields
and the green grass burns
and burns
and burns
bright as a search angel.

Toni Thomas lives in Portland, Oregon. Her poems have been published in Austria, Spain, New Zealand, Canada, England, Scotland, and Australia. In the United States her work has appeared in over fifty literary magazines including *Prairie Schooner, North Dakota Quarterly, Hayden's Ferry Review, the Minnesota Review, Notre Dame Review, Poetry East*, and more. She has published eight collections of poetry and two children's books.

Her figurative clay sculptures have been shown in gallery exhibits in Portland and Chicago, displayed in literary magazines, and housed in private collections in the U.S. and England.

Her short documentary *One of Us* was shown at the Trans-ideology: Nostalgia festival in Berlin and at the Museum of Contemporary Art in Taipei.

Since Toni loves to create and sits buried in reams of poems, stories and manuscripts….she likes to imagine all of them out in the world, swaying wild as lupine.

tonithomaspoetry.com

www.ingramcontent.com/pod-product-compliance
Lightning Source LLC
Chambersburg PA
CBHW030453010526
44118CB00011B/923